# AMELIA EARHART

## DISCOVER THE LIFE OF AN AMERICAN LEGEND

Don McLeese

Rourke

**Publishing LLC**

Vero Beach, Florida 32964

www.rourkepublishing.com

PHOTO CREDITS: All photos Library of Congress

Cover: *Portrait of Amelia Earhart*

Editor: Frank Sloan

Cover design by Nicola Stratford

**Library of Congress Cataloging-in-Publication Data**

McLeese, Don.
  Amelia Earhart / Don McLeese.
    p. cm. — (Discover the life of an American legend)
Summary: A biography of the female aviator who was the first woman to fly alone across the country.
Includes bibliographical references and index.
  ISBN 1-58952-301-6 (hardcover)
  1. Earhart, Amelia, 1897-1937—Juvenile literature. 2. Women air pilots—United States—Biography—Juvenile literature. 3. Air pilots—United States—Biography—Juvenile literature. [1. Earhart, Amelia, 1897-1937. 2. Air pilots. 3. Women—Biography.] I. Title. II. American legends (Vero Beach, Fla.)

  TL540.E3 M38 2002
  629.13'092—dc21

                                        2002004096

Printed in the USA

w/w

# TABLE OF CONTENTS

# WHATEVER BOYS DO

When she was growing up, Amelia Earhart believed that girls should be able to do anything boys could do. Instead of playing with dolls, she loved adventure. After Charles **Lindbergh** became the first **pilot** to fly an airplane across the **Atlantic Ocean** in 1927, Amelia wanted to become the first woman to do so.

*Amelia was a brave girl.*

# LIVING IN KANSAS

Amelia was born on July 24, 1897, in Atchison, Kansas. Her father, Edwin, was a lawyer in Kansas City, Kansas. Her mother, Amy, was the daughter of a judge, one of the richest men in Atchison. Amelia spent the winters with her grandparents in Atchison and her summers with her parents in Kansas City.

*Amelia's home in Atchison, Kansas*

# MILLIE AND PIDGE

Amelia had a younger sister, Muriel. Because Muriel had trouble saying "Amelia," she called her sister "Millie" or "Meelie." Everyone called Muriel "Pidge." The Earhart sisters weren't like the other girls in Atchison. Instead of wearing frilly dresses, they liked to climb trees and play sports like baseball and football.

# FIRST PLANE

In 1908, Amelia and her family moved to **Des Moines**, Iowa. Her father had taken a job there as a railroad lawyer. She went to the Iowa State Fair when she was 10 years old. There she saw her very first airplane. She didn't think much about it at the time. "It was a thing of rusty wire and wood and not at all interesting," she remembered.

*An early airplane*

# MOVE TO CALIFORNIA

As a grown-up, she moved to California in 1920, after her parents did. She and her father went to an **air show** with flying airplanes in Long Beach. This time, the airplanes seemed a lot more interesting to Amelia. After one of them swooped by her, she said, "I believe that little red airplane said something to me."

# FLYING LESSONS

Amelia wanted to be a pilot, so she saved her money for lessons. In 1922, she bought her first plane. She named it "The Canary." She flew 14,000 feet (4,267 meters) into the air. At that time, this was the highest any woman had flown. She also had some accidents, because airplanes weren't as safe then as they are now.

*The inside of an early airplane*

# FIRST WOMAN

After Lindbergh's flight, Amelia was asked to be the first woman to fly across the Atlantic Ocean. She said, "Yes!" The only problem was that she would be a passenger, not the pilot. On June 18, 1928, she flew from **Nova Scotia** to **Wales** across the Atlantic, a trip that made her famous.

*Charles Lindbergh was the first to fly across the Atlantic.*

# ON HER OWN

Amelia wouldn't be happy until she'd flown a plane across the ocean as the pilot. On May 20, 1932, exactly five years after Lindbergh's flight, she flew to **Ireland** all by herself! When she got there, she landed in an open field. A man saw her and asked, "Have you come far?" "From America!" she replied.

# LAST FLIGHT

After a number of long flights, Amelia wanted to fly all the way around the world. She started in June, 1937. She flew 22,000 miles (35,404 kilometers) and only had 7,000 miles (11,265 kilometers) to go. Then her plane disappeared.

Amelia's plane probably crashed into the ocean, but it was never found. The mystery made Amelia even more famous. The brave woman became a legend.

# GLOSSARY

**air show** (AYR SHO) — an event with airplanes flying

**Atlantic Ocean** (at LAN tick OH shun) — the large body of water that separates Europe and Africa from North and South America.

**Des Moines** (deh MOYN) — capital city of Iowa.

**Ireland** (IRE lund) — island west of Great Britain.

**Lindbergh** (LIND burg), Charles — first pilot to fly across the Atlantic Ocean.

**Nova Scotia** (NO vuh SCO shuh) — province in the southeast of Canada.

**pilot** (PIE lut) — person in charge of flying an airplane.

**Wales** (WAYLS) — southwestern part of Great Britain.

# INDEX

## Further Reading

Connolly, Sean. *Amelia Earhart*. Heinemann Library, 2000.
Devillier, Christy. *Amelia Earhart*. ABDO Publishing Company, 2002.
Gormley, Beatrice. *Amelia Earhart: Young Aviator*. Simon & Schuster Children's, 2000.

## Websites To Visit

http://www.ameliaearhart.com

## About The Author

Don McLeese is an award-winning journalist whose work has appeared in many newspapers and magazines. He is a frequent contributor to the World Book Encyclopedia. He and his wife, Maria, have two daughters and live in West Des Moines, Iowa.